for Grandma Jo and
Grammy Sue.

Copyright © 2023 Tia Batten
All rights reserved.

Billy the Bubble

Way out in the ol' wet West,

past the sliver of soap and around
the loofah, lived a bad bubble.

Some might say he was the baddest bubble of them all.

This bad bubble's name was...

BILLY THE BUBBLE

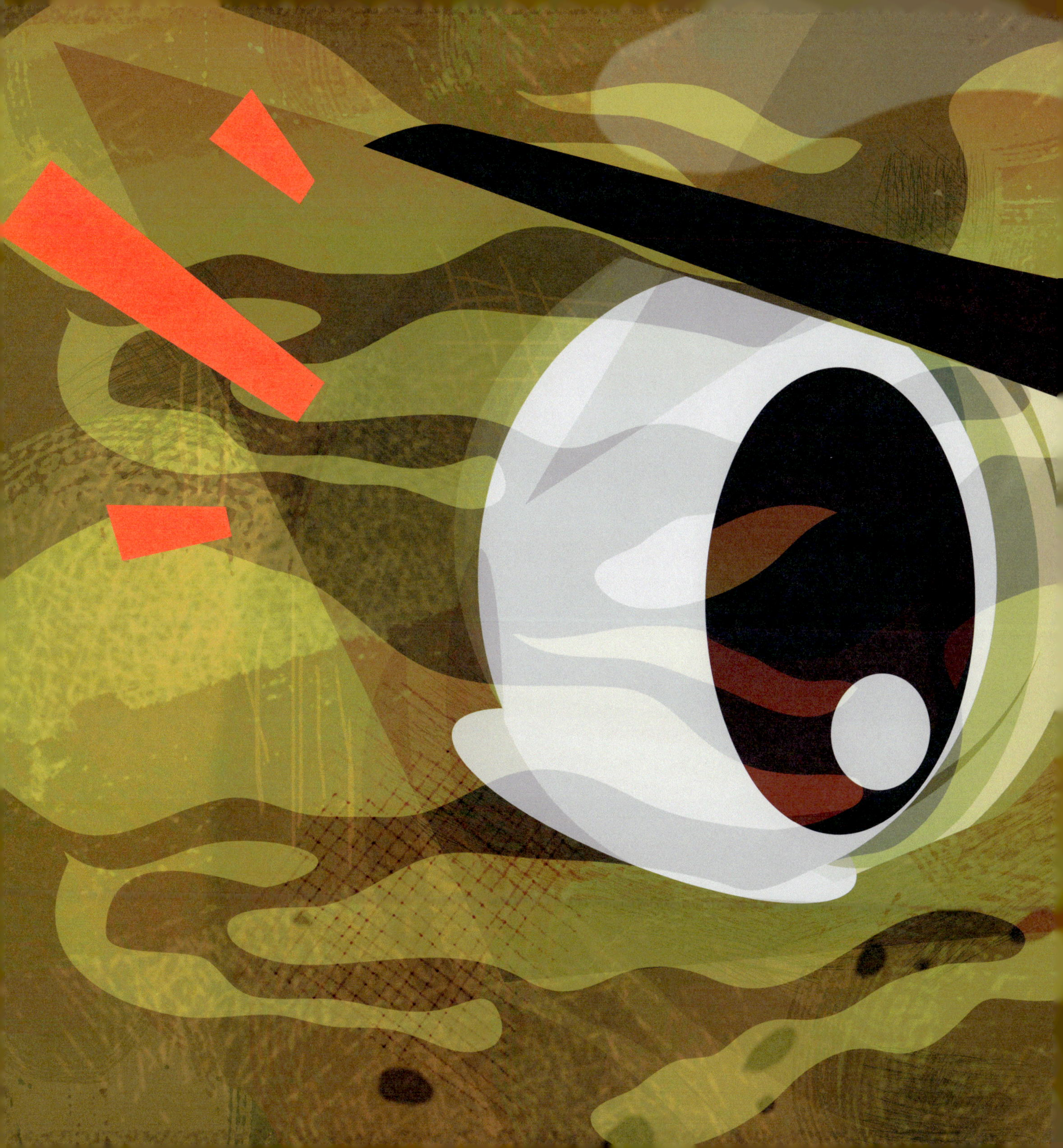

Now,
Billy used to be a nice bubble,

Who was kind
 to the other citizens of Tubville.

But one day, he got mixed in

with a bit of dirt and grime,
and he turned bad.

Ever since, Billy only did bad bubble things.

Like dunking all the bath toys.

Stealing suds from the bubble bank.

And squirting the pirates
on their ship with his squirt gun.

Billy the Bubble
had turned into a real meanie.

The good people of Tubville were afraid of Billy,
and no one knew how to stop him.

One day, Billy came bobbing through Tubville on his rubber ducky.

He swished and splashed until water flew right out of Tubville and straight onto Tiletown.

All the citizens of Tubville hurried away to hide.

The squirty fish swam into
a cup at the bottom of the tub.

The pirate ship floated behind a mountain of suds near the Ol' Leaky Faucet.

And the baby shark?
Well, he didn't know what to do.

Billy tipped back his hat, looked around and laughed.
Tubville was his! Or so he thought.

What Billy didn't realize was that there was a new toy in town.

Sheriff Pops, The Octopus.

Sheriff Pops didn't like how
Billy the Bubble was bullying his town.

He decided he needed to put an end
to Billy Bubble's bad behavior.

"Billy," Sheriff Pops shouted as he crept down from the shower curtain.

"You need to stop your
bad bubble behavior."

Billy pulled his rubber duck to a halt.
"Woah, Ducky."

He bounced off his duck and floated towards Sheriff Pops.

"Yeah?" Billy said.
"What are you gonna do 'bout it?"

"I'd hate to burst your bubble, Billy,
but I think it's time for you to move along.

Now, you can either clean up your act or you can float on over to Toilet Town,"

Sheriff Pops told the bad bubble.

Billy splashed Pops. "No, I'm thinkin'
I'll stay right here."

Then that bad bubble laughed.

Sheriff Pops wiped the
water from his face. "No. You've got to go."

He wriggled forward on his tentacles.
"Cus this tub ain't big enough for the both of us."

Then, just as Billy the Bubble pulled out his squirt gun, planning to squirt Sheriff Pops a tentacle came up and POP!

The grimy bubble was gone,

and in his place was a smaller, squeaky clean bubble.

Billy the Bubble wasn't a bad bubble after all.
He had just been covered in grime, which made him feel and act bad!

With the grime gone,
Billy the Bubble was back to his old, kind self.

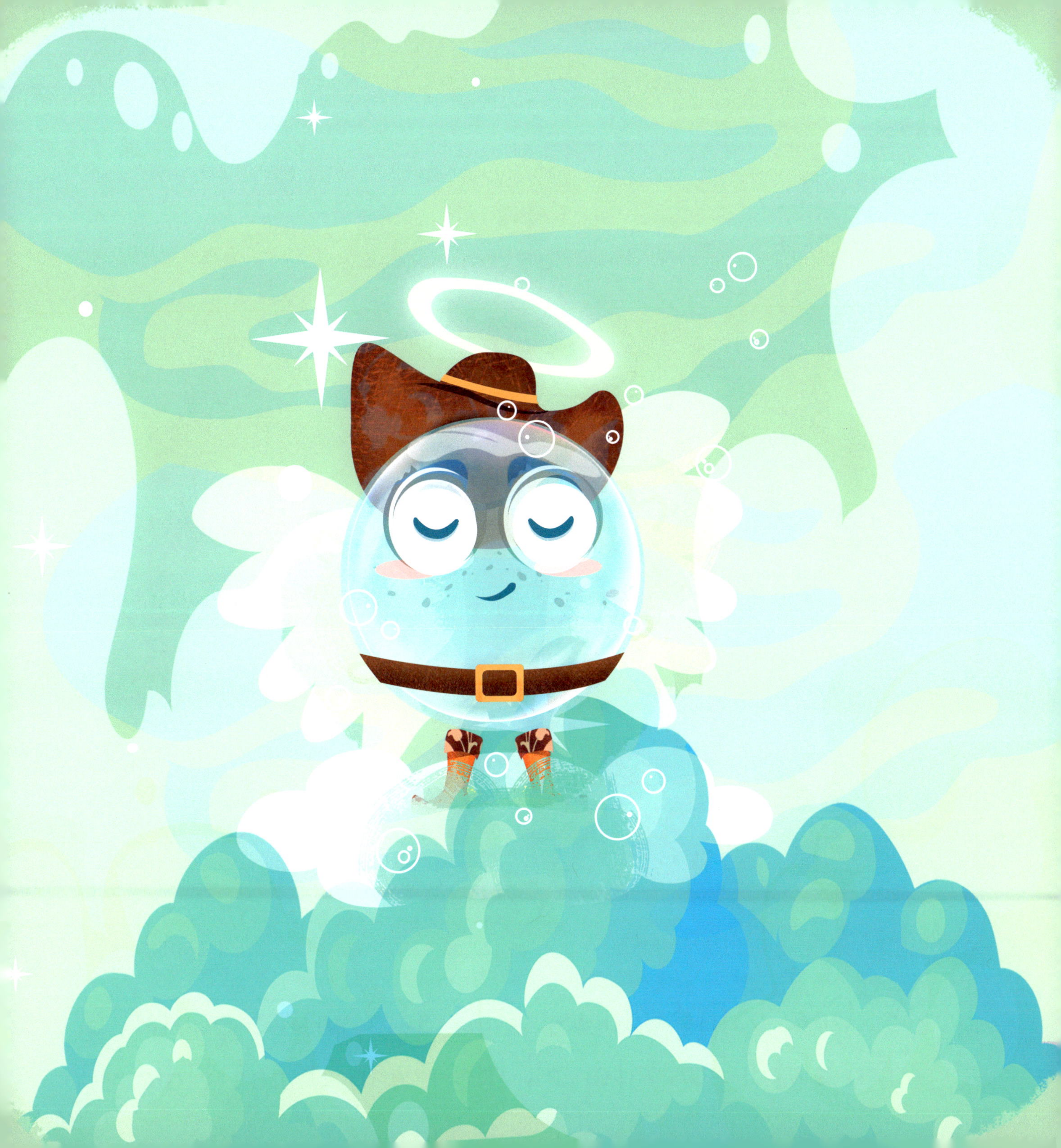

"Gee, bath buddies," Billy said with a pout,
"I'm awful sorry for all the mean things I did.

Can you ever forgive me?"

One by one, the Tubvillians emerged from their hiding spots.

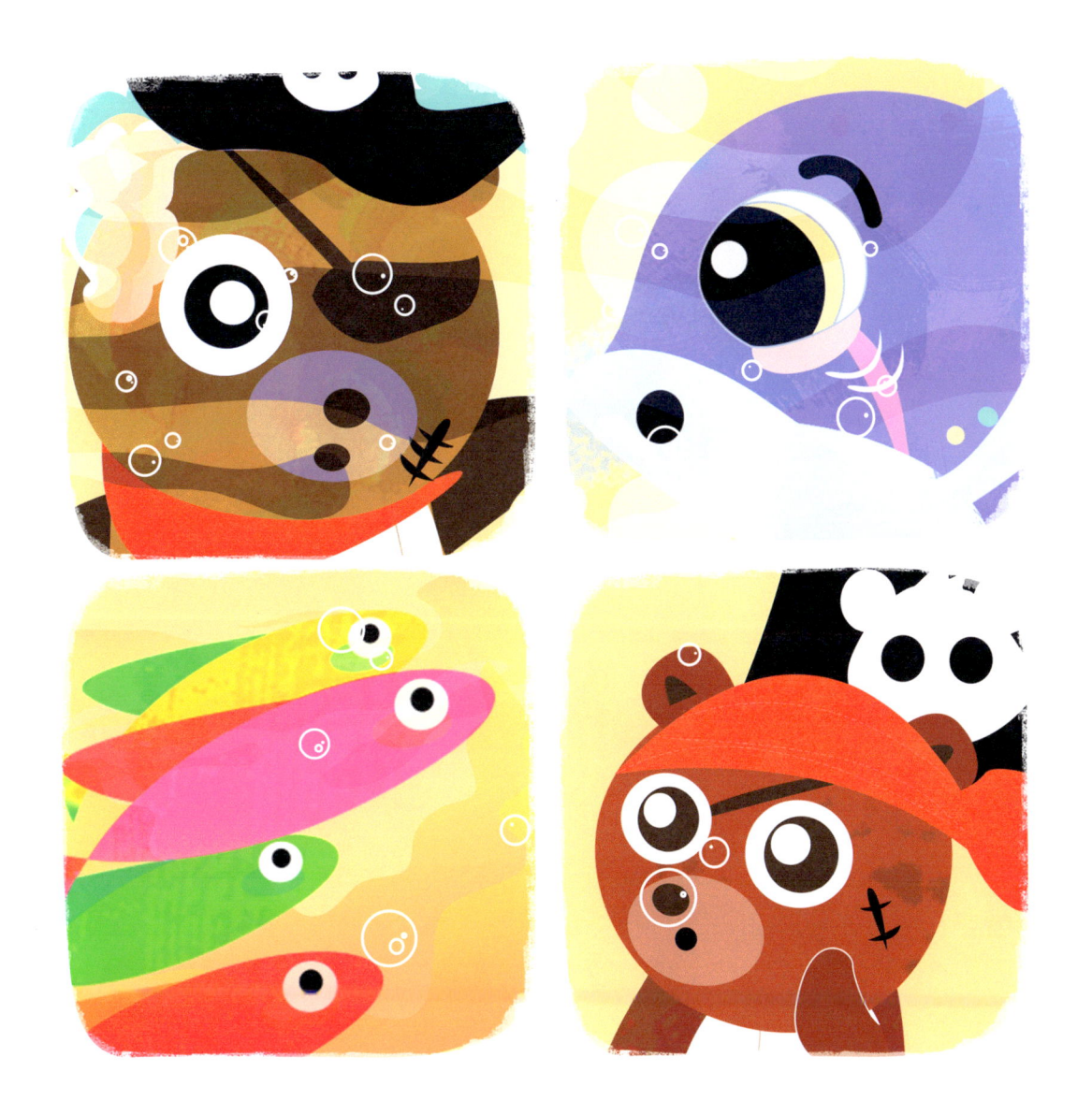

The squirty fish, the soapy pirates and the baby shark all looked at each other.

Then they said, "Of course we forgive you, Billy!" Everyone cheered, and together, they celebrated that their old friend, Billy the Bubble was back to being the best bubble buddy around.

Made in the USA
Columbia, SC
14 December 2024